HOPE IS COMING

Kathryn Epps

FIERY HEDGE POETRY

HOPE IS COMING

First published 2021 by Fiery Hedge Publications

ISBN 978-0-9930473-7-4

Cover design and photography by Kathryn Epps assisted by Lewes Epps

Printed by kindle direct publishing

Kathryn Epps

HOPE IS COMING

<u>Contents</u>

*For my parents, Nick and Christine Ware -
small recompense for years of love and nurture
but given with much love and gratitude*

COME WHAT MAY

Let this be a year of darkness shattered,
a year of hope renewed and answered prayer.
Let our deepest fears be uncovered
so we can face the truth, free from despair.
And let this be a year of *come what may*.

Let this be a year for everyone,
and let our endless striving not be futile.
Grant us the grace to someday love again,
reaching out to others all the while.
And let this be a year of *come what may*.

May this be the year I learn to be.
Restore to me my voice, lost long ago.
Help me fit the role that you intend for me,
and lead me along the paths that I must go.
And let this be a year of *come what may*.

Let this be the year we say *goodbye* no more,
but face the world together, side by side.
And let peace reign our household ever more.
Always in your embrace will I abide.
And let this be the year of *come what may*.

WHEN I LOOK AT THE CROSS

When I look at the cross, I see
graffitied, all the lies I told,
the excuses I made, and the
obscenities I screamed in
anger and frustration.
Then there are the callous names I
called that girl at school;
the things I muttered about my colleague
behind her back. I wince to see the
sexual immorality, scrawled crudely
across the bare wood.
Worst of all are the
bloodstains, from the times I
pushed you away; when you
grazed your hands and side as you
fell to the floor. Even then, I saw
only love in your eyes.
I scrub the cross all day,
until my hands are black
with grime that seems permanently
tattooed to the wood. I wash it with water and bleach,
and then my own tears of anguish and grief,
until you tell me to stop; take my
hands, make me look into
your eyes, still full of love.
I look back at the cross, still dirty and obscene.
But when I look down at my hands,
they are clean.

BLURRED PHOTOGRAPH

for Timothy

The first photograph of you is blurred,
but that seems fitting:
my own memories of the day
are somewhat hazy.
No labour pains preceded your sudden arrival,
just hours spent attached to a monitor,
listening to your heartbeat, and
waiting for the doctors to make a decision.
We thought there would be longer still to wait,
hours, days even, before we'd see your face.
So certain were we of delay that
your dad went back for my hospital bag
which we had stupidly left at home.

That was the moment your heart rate accelerated,
that the doctors felt intervention was necessary,
that I was gowned, and frantically calling your dad,
urging him to return before I was sedated from the waist down.
I didn't want him to miss all the action.
Thankfully the moment of your coming was delayed,
and he returned, dressed in scrubs of blue,
long before your first cry. Or so it seemed.
All sense of time was lost on us.

I lay there, screened from my lower half by a curtain;
strangely detached from it all; movement a distant
notion while the surgeons "washed the dishes" in my belly.
All my preconceptions of birth were dissipated then;
helpless to do anything, my whole being
strained in anticipation of your first cry, the first tears forming
in agonising suspense.

Which fell with the doctors' greetings of "Happy birthday"
as your voice resounded for the first time,

bewildered, bedraggled, all preconceptions of life
beyond the womb dissipated
in that moment.

SECOND; NO LESS

for Guinevere

The second time round,
we knew what to expect;
we were more relaxed,
we'd been there before
under more intense circumstances
than these.

This time round,
we were thoroughly briefed,
we'd been preparing for weeks;
I had time to read the disclaimer
before I signed.

The pain was minimal,
the fear hardly there;
the ambience calm,
tinged with joyful expectation.

You may be the second,
but your coming was no less
momentous; you are no less
significant; you are no less
loved and delighted in.

RECOMPENSE

Once I stayed up all night, administering fluids to
a dehydrated guinea pig; my brother's, it's fair to
note. Said guinea pig lived another five years. I
was the family vet back then; guinea pig diagnostics
a speciality of mine.

Once I bought lunch for a Big Issue seller, besides a
copy of his wares. As a student, the money was
intended for a more selfish purchase, but I knew
where my next meal was coming from;
he didn't.

Once I helped a friend in need; emptied a sink full of
putrid water; and cleared a whole host of plates and
mugs, furry with age. We went out for lunch; then,
afterwards, other duties calling, I said goodbye; left
her in her empty home, while I returned
to mine.

Once I mourned for a man I did not know, but who was
known and loved by a friend of mine. Afterwards, I held
her, my heart breaking for her; my own tears falling with
hers; crying for her loss,
not my own.

Once I cared for the sick.
Once I fed the hungry.
Once I helped someone in need.
Once I comforted those in mourning.

These few things I have done in remembrance of all of you;
who I know have already, unfailingly, done the same for me.

TEACH US TO PLAY

Our child, who art at play,
innocent be thy state.
Thy imagination come,
thy dreams be fulfilled
at home and in the world.
Give us this day the chance to join in,
forgiving us our ignorance
and reluctance to enter fully into your games.
Lead us not into the temptation to be busy
but deliver us from our distractions.
Thine is the freedom, the enjoyment and the wonder
for now and the whole of your childhood.

Oh child, please teach us to play.

HALF REMEMBERED

for Tim Ware

I think I remember you. But then
again, what I take to be memory
amounts to little more than a
photograph on top of the piano,
old video footage that resurfaces
from time to time, when we are
feeling sentimental, and extracts
from my dad's poetry that resonate
with me.

In this half-remembered state, you
remain, therefore, a mystery: the
uncle lost tragically when *he* was
twenty-seven, and I was three. I
suppose I appreciate you all the
more for this sense of the unknown.

I sometimes wonder what you'd mean to
me if you were still alive today; how time
and experience might have shaped you
as it has shaped the rest of us. Certainly,
one big difference would be my firstborn's
name. If you were here, he'd be called
some name other than yours, though
what I cannot fathom; he has made your
name his own.

The children are too young to understand,
but one day I'll pass on all I know of you;
point out your face in family pictures, so
that if you're not remembered for a further
generation, then your name will still be
recalled.

Over the years my fear of death has been consoled by the knowledge that you are already in the next dimension ahead of me. And though my welcome committee's swelled since your passing, it's still a hope of mine that when I arrive, you'll be amongst the first to meet me.

CHILDISHNESS

A rabbit sits in a minute red chair
eating imaginary breakfast from
the plastic bowl and spoon set
before it; while another reclines
in the centre of the table with a
real carrot purloined from the fridge.

The living room carpet is an expressway
for all vehicles imaginable; fire engines,
buses, bin lorries, combine harvesters
and Thunderbirds all plot their aimless
course to an unplanned destination
across the room, harmless collisions inevitable.

A teepee indoors on a rainy day is an excellent
venue for a camping expedition, complete
with a plastic campfire, the detachable flame
slotted into logs which do not smoulder,
the light off and the curtains closed to
represent night; a single lantern, the only comfort.

The social calendar is full: there are doll's tea
parties to attend, a metropolis to build
from bricks with no cement; soft toys to take
care of, babies to dress, play dough banquets,
castles to construct from mud and sand,
leaves and pine cones to collect and treasure.

We perceive their world as small, but really it is
broader by far than ours, that we have confined
by the narrowest limitations, dreams dumbed
down by the painful experience of reality. Theirs
is an age which seldom conforms to expectations
other than their own. For them nothing is impossible.

When we grow weary of their games, we insist

that they grow up, dismissing their notions as
childishness, pretending insult, when really,
we recognise this state as a temporary gift,
a short-lived sacredness, taken away too
soon, never to return again.

THE PERFORMANCE OF MY LIFE

I'm standing on the back of a horse; one leg outstretched,
the other foot feeling for a hold on the curvature beneath
while my hands pump the air with a rhythmic ferocity,
snatching and tossing in turn to keep the balls in motion.
And all the while the audience watches with a mixture of awe
and suspense, holding their applause, for fear that I should

miss a beat

and so send the whole act tumbling comically to the sawdust

below.

Behind the mask, my face is flushed from the heat of their

gaze.

I stand alone in the spotlight that was never wanted.

Seemingly in control, I juggle the school run, balance meal
preparations against home learning activities, and clown
around wearily, supplying entertainment on demand. There is
the inevitable showdown with my youngest, her outburst an

attraction

drawing unwelcome attention, as, like a lion-tamer, I stand

with a

chair's breadth between us, coaxing until her roars subside,

and

she comes to me meekly. We go our way without applause,
merely murmurs, whether real or imagined, as the onlookers

disperse.

Later, my oldest returns to the ring; a runaway horse,

heedless of the

people that clamour around us, impartial to my whispered

warnings

of the potential dangers ahead, but charges on, I in his wake,
his own agenda always to be first. I pirouette, turn a series

of somersaults,

feeding the family, washing the children, further clowning

around before

folding them safely into their beds; then simultaneously

stacking

the dishwasher, wiping surfaces, quietly shutting down the
show

for the night; preparing for the next performance tomorrow.
My grand finale: getting to the bottom of the washing pile.

I'm standing on the back of a horse; one leg outstretched,
the other foot feeling for a hold on the curvature beneath
while my hands pump the air with a rhythmic ferocity,
snatching and tossing in turn to keep the balls in motion.

Or I might as well be. My life is a sideshow in itself.
Roll up, roll up. Come and see the performance of my life.

SUPERWOMAN

They call her superwoman;
she is a highly functioning
individual who runs on
caffeine and power naps.
She has a side-kick
with a tendency to get
into scrapes, but she
loves him and couldn't
do without him all the same.
Superwoman doesn't sleep;
she rights wrong all through
the night. By day she flies about
with unending strength
and unwearying spirit,
yielding to the needs
of those around her
at all costs to her own.
Her arch nemesis is the
feeling of inadequacy,
which dogs her relentlessly,
along with the super villain,
Low Self Esteem,
that preys on her
when she least expects, and
at times threatens to shoot
her out of the sky.
In rare moments of privacy
she unmasks to reveal
bloodshot eyes rimmed
by the darkest shadows,
lips set in grim determination:
the face of another tired mum.
Still superwoman, just minus the
superpowers, and by no means
invincible.

DEAR DICK

Your side-kick's loyalty is questionable;
he snickers behind his paws at your every failure.
He doesn't really expect your dastardly deeds to succeed.
Perhaps, like me, he feels your efforts would be better
                                                    channelled
into racing, rather than tripping up the competition.
But then, if you haven't realised this yourself
after seventeen races then I fear
you never will.

FEAR OF THE UNKNOWN

There is an unknown person
from an unknown place
living in my village;
an incomer,
probably with ill intent and plans to change
the way things are done around here.
For we've heard they're anti-social
and prone to criminal behaviour,
the like of which no one born and bred here
would ever undertake.
We must close our doors to them,
narrow the inner circle,
making it clear they will never belong here,
no matter how long they remain.

There is an unknown person
from an unknown country
living in ours;
an immigrant,
perhaps to take what they can get
and send it back home to their families.
For we've heard they'll take our jobs
and our benefits,
and force their ways, their views upon us.
We must close the borders,
turn them away, send them packing,
no matter what they're fleeing from.

There is an unknown virus
from an unknown source
sweeping across my country;
an invader,
surely to bring us doom.
For we've heard that people have died
and no doubt we'll be next.
We must plunder the supermarkets,

stripping the shelves bare
lest we find ourselves under siege.
No matter if there's nothing left for others.

I am an unknown person
living in an unknown village
in an unknown country
at risk of an unknown virus.
Will no one have compassion on me?

LIVING PROOF

Living: Reduces the life-span by sixty seconds per minute.

How do we live when all that we do bears an impact
on ourselves,
on others,
on the world around us?

Do we contemplate each step with care, or do we charge on,
oblivious to who or what we hurt
along the way?

Do we prioritise cost and convenience,
or do we make the effort to practise ethics
and fair trade?

Do we take care of ourselves,
or do we in our haste
bring on self-harm?

Do we walk past the undesirable,
or do we risk offering a hand of friendship
and warmth?

Do we insist on an eye for an eye,
or do we bravely, defiantly
turn the other cheek?

Do we declare war to attain our demands,
or do we sacrifice them to
make way for peace?

Do we follow in the careless footsteps of our ancestors,
or do we, through considerate living, become proof
that we are capable of change?
And in doing so change the world for the better.

OK

Two letters big enough for us to hide behind;
like a smile that doesn't reach the eyes
conveys reassurance until met with scrutiny.

We can cover all traces of tears shed behind closed doors
and act the part of someone carefree,
never once alluding to the internal aching abyss
that feeds on our grief, our shame, our fear;
the imperative voice that tells us
this is something that cannot be shared.

It's the stigma we fear: the label
staining our foreheads in permanent marker;
the change of perspective we expect
from the people around us, the loss of credibility.
We assume they'll always think us
fragile, incapable, unstable;
that this makes us less than who we are.

It's easier to hide behind OK, than to admit
my life is falling apart,
I feel so lost
I want to end it all.

It takes far more of ourselves to utter the truth:
I am not OK.

But I promise you, that if you let me know
I will help you make it all OK
I will not rest until you are OK.

THE WHEEL BARROW

I am the wheel barrow,
circumnavigating the narrowest course
with one wheel where
two should ease the strain.

The load exceeds full capacity;
my spirits strewn mercilessly
across the path with every jolt,
my will struggling over each rut.

I heed not the birdsong
nor the compassionate sun
that evaporates
the icy glaze within.

I see only a destination
to which I am called,
the relief to be found,
though temporary,
when so much depends upon me.

HOPE IS COMING

Blue sky in a puddle.
A baby's face creased with laughter.
Warmth from the winter sun transcending the Arctic wind.
Hope is coming.

Solace found in a brimming teacup.
Daffodils awakening from a bed of snow.
Exchanging smiles with a passing stranger.
Hope is coming.

A church illuminated by candlelight.
The rumble of a passing storm overhead.
An owl hooting beyond canvas walls.
Hope is coming.

A cluster of stars blazing the blackest of nights.
The satisfaction of a hard day's work well done.
The blissful state between wakefulness and sleep.
The blessing of a new day waiting in the dawn.
Hope is coming.

FAMILY IN LOCKDOWN

The days start early; sometimes it's before six
when our five-year-old son climbs into bed for
a cuddle. I sense on some level he's reassuring
himself that we're still there. With all the changes
wrought in the last few weeks, there's room for doubt.

My watch stopped three weeks before the outbreak;
I never got around to getting the battery replaced
before lockdown came into effect. Clock-watching
is still a habit of mine, perhaps more so now,
though no longer a necessity. My vigil serves
to maintain some structure to days that threaten to
drift aimlessly, into oblivion.

It's not all bad. There's more time to invest in
hobbies and household projects. We ticked
scarecrow-making off the children's bucket list,
and the long dreamed of herb garden
flourishes on the kitchen window sill; I now
have an abundance of thyme on my hands.

Though we miss our family, friends and neighbours,
our social lives have never been better;
technology makes the absences
easier to bear, bridging the gap between
communities cut off by pestilence. We attend church
and theatre performances from our living room,
becoming more cultured by the day.

Books are a comfort, with their ability to transport
a soul confined to homestead, across
the parameters of space and time,
and into another world entirely. In recent weeks
I've frolicked on Prince Edward Island,
solved crime in rural Norfolk, and experienced
isolation on another scale in the middle of the North Sea.

I find myself increasingly dependent on this form of escapism
in a reality where we haven't left the house in
more than a month.

Snapshots of life caught on camera
show glimpses of a family that's
mercifully happy and healthy. We keep no visual
evidence of the difficult days, where the children
transpose into wild things, and the uncertainty
weighs heavily upon us all. But the tears
wash away in the shower, and we hold to
the pledge that tomorrow's a new day;
that one day the present situation
will be past tense, a piece of history we were a part of;
something to tell the grandchildren about.

HUMAN SHIELD

Protecting you,
not by standing between you
and the gunfire,
but removing myself from the battle
to stay at your side;
surrendering my independence,
submitting to house arrest,
remaining here indefinitely,
a prisoner of war.

They call it shielding,
implying heroism, sacrifice,
rather than the helplessness I feel.

THE THINGS THAT HAVEN'T CHANGED

April, and the garden is yellow
with dandelions; the children
pull them up in handfuls and
thrust them into jam jars,
bringing colour into the house,
much as they did last spring.
The weeds are still persistent,
but now I am freer to keep them
in check; the wilderness is
gradually being tamed. From
the windows I watch the
comings and goings of the
birds, gleaning all that's been
uprooted and discarded, the
perfect spoils for nest-making.
They are constantly busy,
winter over for them at last,
while our hibernation has only
just begun. The first of the
summer migrants appear, and
I watch with envy as they soar
high and free against the clear
sky. We just about know what
day we're on, but the calendar
has never been emptier. The
days pass by and the seasons
will come and go, but the
passage of time for us has
altered. And so life goes on, as
do we, grasping for the familiar
in a world gone strange, taking
comfort in the things that haven't
changed.

I DIDN'T KNOW

When I promised to love you from this day forward, I didn't
    know so much was set to change.
When I promised to love you for better, for worse, I didn't
    know there would be times ahead where our world
    would feel fragile and threatened.
When I promised to love you for richer, for poorer, I didn't
    know that finances would be the least of our worries.
When I promised to love you in sickness and in health, I
    didn't know your health could hold me captive in our home.
When I promised to love you until death do us part, I didn't
    know that one day I would shield your life by giving up
    mine.

But

before we met, I didn't know the joy of uniting my life with
    another and collaborating to create something beautiful,
    illuminating, wondrous.
I didn't know that sacrifice was something I could make so
    willingly, that I would be repaid in love collateral.
I didn't know that if the future was laid bare before us on
    our wedding day, my response would still be the same.
Because it has all been worth it.
Your love was always enough.

DIRGE FOR THE LOST GENERATION

Eat, drink and be merry; the world is your
oyster after all. Gather ye rosebuds
and trample them underfoot; someone else
will pay the bill. Wrap the world in plastic,
raze the trees, belch your endless fumes into
the atmosphere; graze the ozone layer,
damage irreparably and cast all
creatures out into the quiet realm of
extinction. Muddy the waters, poison
the seas; use all resources to the full.
And in the end return to dust in peace;
leave behind a lasting legacy to
a new generation, now out of luck,
born into a world that's already fucked.

AFTER HUMANKIND

It takes no time for the earth to move on from us
when time itself has become obsolete; there's
no one left to measure the progress of the sun and
moon.

The bare bones of tarmac are quickly erased
by the layers of foliage that have formed, like new
flesh over a wound to create a living, breathing
freeway.

The skeletons have long since crumbled into dust;
and the tower blocks collapsed and claimed
by the vegetation; new formations, accidental
mountains.

The silence is the greatest wonder to behold
in a world more beautiful now there's no one left
to spoil her; but equally desolate, now that no one
remains to enjoy her.

THE WIND TURBINE'S ADDRESS

They say we're a blot on the landscape,
eyesores, our arms outstretched,
orbiting, obscuring their picture-perfect
view. What they don't appreciate is that
we're here to help clean up the mess
they've already made of their planet.
We are man-made mechanisms,
designed to catch the wind and convert it
into energy. If they had taken more care
in the first place, then perhaps there would
be no need for us now. We would cease to be
anything more than imagery from a dystopian
future: of a nation rapidly running out of
resources; a world damaged beyond repair.

Please accept that though our occupation
mars the view, we're really buying back
the time that's been squandered through
careless living. With each rotation we're
renewing life, and circulating the good news
that with us the future's still a possibility.

MARK MAKING

Trees grow from the eroded river bank,
roots exposed by the water's graceful flow,
gradually altering its shape and course,
effortlessly sculpting a new tomorrow.
The tree limbs hang tirelessly in midair
and from their branches, here and there,
dangle alien fruits in lurid hues,
fruits that do not decompose,
rippling faintly in the breeze.
The forest floor is another metaphor
for this merging of two worlds:
the expected flotsam of roots and leaves,
feathers, sticks and stones intermingles
with discarded Strongbow cans,
cigarette butts and empty crisp packets.
Further along, Connor and Lacey
have marked their territory like dogs,
their names streaked across trees
in pink spray paint, a permanent tattoo,
their ownership implied.

This place is beautiful,
but we have left our mark.

AN OASIS FOR BEES

This garden is barren;
all bare earth and concrete
besides the usual semblance
of unwelcome weeds.
The few flowers it yields
are quickly pulled up by
eager children, and little
remains for a bee to suck.

But still the bees come,
finding nourishment
where we thought none,
and should they succumb
to thirst, we revive them
with saucers of sugared water,
watching over them until
they take to noisy flight.

We ourselves know the desert
and have drunk deep
from the wells of kindness
flowing closer to the surface
than we once thought.
Now aspiring to be an oasis
to others, we welcome all;
not forsaking a bee in need.

RE-ENTRY

Five months is a long time to be away.
At times our home has felt as far removed
from the world as a space station in orbit,
two hundred and twenty miles or more
beyond human contact, but always awaiting
further instruction from mission control.

It was harder still when we watched the world
below seemingly return to normality
in some shape and form, while we ourselves
continued in suspended animation,
lost in transition, and constantly gravitating
towards the airlock where the escape pod sat.

Finally, ground control got through,
and we prepared for our re-entry,
making the adaptations necessary
to survive on a planet that's somewhat
altered in our absence. Happy to report,
now we've made the descent, I'm not breaking up yet.

BEHIND THIS MASK

Initially I felt restricted, almost suffocated
by the fabric compressing my nose and mouth,
my breath warm, sauna-like, misting my
glasses to conceal the new world I'm merging into.

Later comes the realisation that behind this mask
my self-consciousness has fallen away.
Strangely, I feel safer, more sure of myself
with my face half covered, like a superhero

which, in a way, I am. I can still smile, still share
moments with those around me, eye contact
playing a fundamental part in these transactions,
where before it was tentative, almost awkward.

And though a part of me is hidden, nothing is lost,
but lives are being saved in the process.

SUMMERING IN THE NORTHERN HEMISPHERE

We look for you in the Spring,
have learned to expect the first
of your kind around mid-April,
or whenever the first of the
blue-sky days should fall;
we spy you skimming overhead,
hear you call laughingly,
as though you have never been away.

You soar, riding the currents above,
or resting momentarily
on telegraph wires, though
never still for long and always
chattering away, seemingly
without any care in the world.
Because for you it is always summer;
you chase the sun's rays around the globe.

A barn or hovel is an adequate place
to squat, to pass the nights quietly
until a noisy family awakens
from their shells, a new generation
of migrants and wayfarers
to follow you South, long before
the nights start to chill and the
leaves brown at the edges.

I can never pinpoint the day you are gone;
you leave without ceremony,
taking to wing without tears or regret.
If you ever feel sorrow
then you hide it well. Should your time
run its course before next we meet
you'll fade out calmly, knowing finally that your
permanent residence is a place of endless sunshine.

THE FIRST TIME YOU FLEW

Were you astonished, the first time you flew,
or even faintly surprised when you spread
your wings and found yourself airborne? Or
was flight not so much a possibility as an
inevitability, a speculation formed from
observing a whole flock of your kind take
to wing in unison, ahead of you? Perhaps
it wasn't even a conscious decision, but
instinct that led you to teeter at the edge
of all you once knew, letting go and
trusting your unpracticed wings to autopilot
upwards before you hit the ground. Now
that you are fully fledged you might not
glance back, the gentlest breeze propelling
you forward into new possibilities. Yet if the
elements pummel you to the ground, don't
be too proud to rest and, once restored,
attempt a second launch into a kinder sky.
Whatever your story, your journey in life, whether
wily gull or resilient puffin,
spirited swallow or reticent corncrake,
territorial blackbird or inquisitive robin,
determined woodpecker or dainty hummingbird,
solitary raven or synchronised starling,
migrating goose or homing pigeon,

I wish you godspeed,
and pray that you will soar.

PENMANSHIP

Whenever I open my mouth the voice
that comes is hesitant and faltering,
each word requiring a conscious effort,
often forgotten mid-sentence, my speech
fragmented, sometimes incomplete. But when
I touch pen to paper, the words flow in
a torrent akin to striking water
from a rock, an everyday miracle,
granting the articulation lacking
in my spoken English, and natural
coherence to my stream of consciousness.
Penmanship is a gift: this compulsion
to write has given me cause to rejoice;
through ink and paper I've at last found my voice.

SEEN AND HEARD

I speak
I call
I shout
in case anyone is listening

I smile
I wave
I gesture
should someone look my way

I offer
I reach out
I make contact
to establish a connection

I live
I participate
I make myself known
to be a part of this story

QUIET AMBITION

I'm not destined to be famous in this life;
the world is never going to know my name.
I won't be remembered in a century's time;
I'll be forgotten in my entirety,
a name etched in the sand
only to be washed away by the tide.
But I think it's better that way;
to fade quietly out of existence
without ceremony, but knowing
I counted for something where it mattered;
thought of in the years to come
only by those who knew me best
and loved me most.

BEING ME

In a world of almost eight billion
originality feels scarce. It's hard
to stand out when the competition is
overflowing to the point of flooding
the drain so you can't even drown yourself
in self-pity. Personally, I've found
it best to let go and stop my striving;
be content with who I am and gently
make my presence known, never forcing my
self upon others, but letting them see
the real me, because that in itself
is beautiful and wonderful indeed.

Keep on shining; if nobody sees you
it's purely that they're blinded by your light.

SELKIE

A part of me feels that I don't belong here,
that I was smuggled here under false pretences,
stripped of my skin and forced to adapt
to this alien world in the form of another.

I pick up the language remarkably well,
my body mimicking their gestures effectively,
and now I am accepted as one of them,
no one suspecting the usurper in their midst.

Sometimes I even fool myself for a time,
until a wave breaks over the rocks,
assailing me with its salty allure,
and the sea song calling me home.

I will myself never to forget where I come from,
and one day I will swim effortlessly away,
my dying breath the bark of a seal;
no longer lost but finally at home in my second skin.

SOMBRE SUNDAY AFTERNOONS

Saturday is hopeful,
but there's always a poignancy,
a tender nostalgia
that comes around mid-afternoon
on a Sunday.

It stems back to childhood,
the anticipation of another
school day dawning
in the rapidly fading light
of a weekend almost over.

It's worse in autumn,
the dwindling daylight cheerless,
and the gloom descending
noticeably sooner
than the week before.

In spring and summer time
it's less prevalent,
softened by sunlight
and the prospect of
long summer holidays ahead.

Even now, as an adult,
I feel the same dull ache within,
the sense of something that's almost over,
although there's nothing left to fear:
Monday is, for me, an additional day of rest.

COLLECTIONS

In spring they gather flowers,
heedless of name or colour,
but drawn by the beauty of the petals.
They take great delight in
every one they find, even
the ones we dismiss as weeds.
We put them in water,
trying to extend a life cut short
by children's hands.

In summer they bring home
shells and pebbles
gleaned from the seashore,
the souvenirs of summer jaunts.
They discern shapes in these
and each has a tale to tell, such as
the "elephant's trunk" hoodwinked from Iona,
and the heart from a South Devon beach.

In autumn they collect leaves
which are then left to disintegrate
in the hall unless we have the foresight
to immortalise them in the flower press.
Later we'll make artwork
from these preserved specimens,
although they themselves represent
the beauty to be found in a season of decay.

In winter they pick up whatever they can find,
the flowers dead, the leaves turned to mush
and the pebbles miles away
on the deserted shores,
but anything found can be a treasure
be it a coin, marble or feather.

Once it was a pink balloon, once a small giraffe;

everything cherished for as long as it will last.

LOOK INTO MY EYES

Look into my eyes.
Do not look around my eyes.
Look only into my eyes.

What do you see?

Two pupils, dilating in the light.
Two irises in myriad colours,
that blend into a single hue
when seen from afar.
White jelly criss-crossed with tiny veins,
the whole effect framed by lids and lashes.

These, supposedly the windows to my soul,
reveal so much of who I am
yet are frequently missed
when the picture is viewed in full.

Instead, what is seen
is a skin colour, gender or age;
not a person
but a stereotype
to be judged and dismissed
without a second glance.

Look into my eyes.
Do not look around my eyes.
Look only in my eyes.

Look past what you perceive
to be surface damage
and see what really matters,
see the spirit dancing within.
Look into my eyes for long enough
and you may fall in love with what you see.

REVITALISING BODY

Ten toes help two soles grip the ground,
while two ankles elevate
the trunk of the body skywards,
two knees bending gently to lower it
back down to earth as required.

Two hips and one pelvis swivel to survey the land,
one torso stretches and projects
the limbs extending from its base:
two arms reaching out,
two hands holding, ten fingers gripping,
nails snagging in desperate measures.

One neck supports the head;
one face looks around with two eyes,
listens with two ears, breathes with one nose,
smiles with two lips, expresses itself
with one tongue, one voice box and ample body language.

One hundred thousand hairs warm the scalp,
offering distinction in their colour and length.

Six hundred and fifty muscles obey
the instruction of one brain, encased inside its skull;
one spine directing each thought process.

One heart pumps the life within,
two lungs circulate the inhalations of the nose,
one digestive system sifts
energy and waste from what is consumed.
Twenty-four ribs enclose and protect,
beneath excess tissue and seven layers of skin.

Two testes and two ovaries manufacture life
through the unity of one male body and one female;
one womb carries life until it can be sustained on earth.

One revitalising body performs for us at will,
an everyday miracle too often taken for granted,
subject to our own abuse and neglect,
yet functioning for a limited time only.
We should take better care of it.

MATURING LOVE

The romance is still there,
just less accessible these days;
buried under
endless to-do lists,
subject to interruption from
our well-meaning offspring,
and liable to nod off
in the evenings.

In thirteen years you've seen me
change from girlish teen
to wife and mother,
and I've watched you
grow into a man
while still retaining
your boyhood charm.
We have a history together.

If anything, we have grown closer
over the years;
the obsessive hand-holding
of our needy youth
giving way to untold intimacy
in our fleeting looks, and
the briefest caresses
made in passing.

We are two trees standing side by side,
branches waving in the wind,
just out of reach,
yet below the surface
our roots are entwined,
anchoring us into rich soil
with confidence that our
maturing love is set to last.

EARLY DAYS OF MULTI-TASKING

A crowded room never felt more lonely
than the church hall toddler group.
I trailed in my small son's wake
across an obstacle course
of toys and clusters of children,
my baby daughter strapped to my chest,
already rooting for its milky source.
I knew, even then, I had set myself up to fail.

Of course, it all ended in tears, not forsaking
my own, my son's cut lip
bearing testimony to his neglect
when I stopped to feed the baby.
But if I was a failure that day, my children
didn't know it, and in the days, weeks, years
that followed, they have flourished
under my loving nurture, never asking for more
than I had to give to them.

A SPHERE OF HIS OWN

I know he isn't being deliberately
naughty; it's just that the magnetic pull
of his own agenda is sometimes stronger
than our entreaties and warnings.

He moves in a sphere of his own,
literally walking in concentric circles,
following the narrow channels cut
between our table and chairs.

In his head he is elsewhere. I hear
snatches of his happy chatter
and secretly wish I could be with him.
Instead, I tell him automatically:

to *sit down while he's eating;*
the sofa's not for walking on;
hold my hand, there's a road ahead;
for the last time, stop doing that.

Always an imperative soaked with guilt
and motherly fear for a child that's different:
fear that I cannot reach him
because I am stuck on planet earth

while he resides always on a higher plane.

THE DAUGHTER FORECAST

Her temperament is good or moderate,
occasionally poor, becoming cyclonic for a time,
later good.

When her opinion is consulted
she's blowing a Southwesterly,
veering Northwesterly,
uttering yes when she means no
and correcting herself in a single breath.

Generally we can expect highs
throughout the day
dissipating into lows
with squally showers around bedtime.

If gale warnings are imminent
we surround our little tempest
with love, riding the storm together
until it gives way to calm once more.

REALLY SEEING

My children wave at road sweepers
and roofers that would otherwise go
unnoticed by my undiscerning eye.

"Look, Mummy, the moon!" they exclaim;
it's the tiniest crescent, barely
visible against the pale blue sky.

They're always looking up, down, all around,
never failing to miss a single thing,
while my gaze falls always downwards,
ever intent upon whatever's beneath my feet.

I wonder when it was that I stopped really seeing,
when the world ceased to be for me a fantastical sight;
when every little thing became less
than something to marvel at.

A BUTTERFLY'S WINGS

for Christina

A butterfly's wings
flutter in a sunflower
as she stops to feed.

They catch the sunlight,
beautiful and delicate,
seemingly fragile.

I see, on closer
inspection, hers are ragged,
yet serviceable,

speaking of profound
resilience, untold strength
within her spirit.

She reminded me
of you; I felt a kinship
with this butterfly

who had been through much,
but continued to flutter
through her course in life;

a true survivor,
sipping nectar, resting in
beds of sunflowers.

PUTTING THE CAMERA TO ONE SIDE

We live in an age where
memory is not enough;
photographic evidence
has become a vital part
of preserving a moment in time,
enabling us to clearly recall
the details that are sometimes lost.

It's become an obsession now, photographs recording
even the trivialities of our day.

We are told to capture it, share it;
but be careful,
a digital image is poor compensation
for life experienced in full.

Memories are precious,
and yet, photographs give us a mere glimpse
of a moment made more sacred
by putting the camera to one side.

Take a picture, by all means;
just don't let the camera dictate.
Live for the moment
rather than commit it to memory.

STREET ENTERTAINMENT

Another summer day in the city;
we saw a man riding a unicycle
whilst simultaneously freeing himself from a straitjacket,
five pound per head the recommended fee
for this impressive feat.

Meanwhile, tucked away and almost
out of sight behind a paperback book,
sits a young man, apparently reading for pleasure,
the cup of loose change and his position
on the pavement indicating that this
is by no means a moment of leisure.

We saw a woman dressed as Yoda,
apparently levitating a foot above the ground;
while another woman huddles in a blanket,
wearing a winter hat on a warm August day,
unable to shake the coldness of the street from her weary
                                                                limbs,
let alone elevate herself
to more favourable climes.

We heard a man singing into a microphone,
strumming an electric guitar,
the music following us all the way down the street;
but more haunting still
is a beggar's appeal for any loose change,
whispered because they're almost
too ashamed to ask;
their voice is immediately lost in the crowd.

Another day in the city
and a multitude of people trying to scratch a living,
some dreaming of their name in lights,
while others facing the prospect
of another cold night under the stars.

WE TREAT THE DEAD BETTER THAN WE DO THE LIVING

We treat the dead better than we do the living,
our visits more regular and ritualistic
now that the conversation's one-sided.
We almost always bring flowers,
leaving them on wood and stone
to go unobserved and unappreciated
until they dry up and are discarded.
We revere our loved ones more
when we speak of them in the past tense;
they become more saintlike now that
their bad habits have died with them,
and we recall them with genuine affection
forgetting the traits that formerly obscured
the regard we had for them.
We make sure they have every comfort in death,
laying them to rest in a prime location
with an enviable view into the great beyond,
and erecting the finest tributes,
preserved in stone for all to see and know.
We treat the dead better than we do the living
because mortality makes us realise
what we take for granted in life,
that which we cling to in death
when it is too late to turn back time,
and, really, we would give anything
to have them back among us,
even for just one day more.

CHOPPING DOWN WOODS ON A SUNNY MORNING

Another day, another ancient tree felled: 300-year-old
Hunningham Oak near Leamington is knocked down to make
way for HS2.
THE NORTHAMPTON CHRONICLE, MONDAY, 28TH
SEPTEMBER, 2020

Whose woods these were I do not know;
the time has come for them to go;
my plans demand this land be clear
to make way for new rail and road.

My conscience seems to think it queer
to tear down what has long been here;
it seems a shame that I should take
away what's stood a hundred years.

It gives me cause to hesitate,
to wonder if there's some mistake
that I should raze this to a heap.
I give my head a solemn shake.

These woods are shady, cool and deep,
but I have targets still to keep
and by tonight the trees will sleep.
And by tonight the trees will sleep.

WE WERE HERE FIRST

It's an argument that seems to work for you
when you feel your habitat is under threat,
so why not *we*
who have been here longer than your forefathers?
We are literally rooted here,
unwilling protestors waiting to be cut down,
unable to put up any resistance against the chainsaws
or even flee in the wake of our death warrant.
A hundred years may seem a lifetime to you,
but we are still in the prime of our lives
at two centuries or more;
there is no need to euthanise us
when we have plenty of life left,
and oxygen to bestow on future generations,
oxygen that you have willingly traded in
for a better transport system.
You have sold out on your children:
pure air for polluted roads,
a busy, hectic landscape
for the tranquility of the forest.
Even if you replace each one of us,
planting saplings in our memory,
you will never live to see them
in all their glory, as we stand today.
Tomorrow when you visit the killing fields
and walk among the bodies of the fallen,
remember for a moment the sanctuary
we once provided: the branches arching overhead
to shelter from the elements,
the soothing whisper of the leaves in the wind,
enough to send you to sleep
against the strong trunk cradling you
like a grandparent, asking for nothing more
than for you to put your arms around them
and hug them tight. We were here first,
but we want to be part of the future too.

MORNING LULL

Early in the morning the teapot beckons.
The children, already awake, are installed
in their beds with books and toys,
while I look, not for further repose,
but the solace of the morning
before the day really begins.

I take my tea looking out across
our south facing garden,
where already the sunlight is reclaiming
what was temporarily engulfed by nocturnal shadows.
Next door's cat keeps watch from the wall,
giving the scene the feel
of a Shirley Hughes picture
in a children's book.

Meanwhile, the birds are up and breakfasting
on the remains of grass seed
sown too late in the season to yield,
killed off by the earliest of frosts.
But from this year's failings
we will reap next year's harvest.

The spell breaks with the final drops
of rapidly cooling tea,
and I resign myself to the busyness of the day,
knowing it'll be over all too soon,
but thankful for this morning lull,
this moment of stillness and quiet;
the calm before the storm.

SUNLIGHT AND SHADOWS

"I want it to be Christmas now!"
It's the lament of a child for whom
this year has yielded one disappointment
after another: no birthday parties,
no family visits, no holidays.
That's not to say there haven't been good times
but these are easy to overlook
when you are four, your skin is writhing with spots
and Christmas is still another ten weeks
away over the horizon.
Judging from social media she's coping
as well as the rest of us,
perhaps better, being at an age where we can distract
her from her complaints relatively easily.

I sometimes wonder if it was selfish of me
to wish her and her brother into this fragile world,
where joy and sorrow are so tightly interlaced,
where discontent often rules our hearts,
blinding us to life's sweetness;
and where one day, in accordance with nature's law
I will be forced to abandon them.

It's in these uncertain times that I realise my mission as
                                                    parent
is to love and nurture, whilst discreetly
preparing them to fend for themselves;
to help them see the sunlight for the shadows,
and reinforce that really this isn't such a bad place to live.
Then perhaps, in my absence, they may be
the blessing to the world that they are to me.

THE WORST ISN'T OVER

The light at the end of the tunnel is dimming,
the numbers are rapidly rising again,
everyone's set on returning to normal,
but we know the worst isn't over yet.

Now that the lockdown restrictions have lifted
they're acting as though the last months never happened,
they've tasted the freedom and there's no going back,
the numbers are rapidly rising again.

They seem unconcerned that the virus is spreading,
they're ignoring the signs that it's gaining control;
though recent history's repeating itself,
everyone's set on returning to normal.

They're putting in measures, too little, too late,
the second wave's here and it's time to go swimming;
mask up, wash your hands if you want to be spared;
the light at the end of the tunnel is dimming.

They've forgotten the limits on hospital beds,
the 42,000 or more that are dead,
and the nights spent applauding our dear NHS,
but we know the worst isn't over yet.

The light at the end of the tunnel is dimming,
the numbers are rapidly rising again,
everyone's set on returning to normal,
but we know the worst isn't over yet.

WHERE TOUCH IS ABSENT AND SMILES GO UNSEEN

In a world where we can no longer
reach out and hold hands,
where it's no longer possible
to pull each other into a supportive embrace,
and where we screen the lower half
of our faces for the benefit of those around us,
I hope you can still hear the smile in my voice.

LOVE IS BEHIND

Love is behind doorstep deliveries of
cake and seeds and willow branches,
unexpected packages of second-hand clothes,
and shopping bags of tins left in a church porch,
the kiss of sunlight on an autumn day,
the glimpse of the harvest moon at dusk.
Love flows from the Father's heart and hands,
presenting itself to us in the gifts of others
and the blessings of the world around us,
never forcing but offering itself
in thoughtful tokens of kindness.

Love is behind the miraculous sunrise
and the awe-inspiring sunset;
shimmering in the early morning dew
and sparkling in the frost;
glowing in the faces around us that
look upon us with compassion and care.
Love shines from the Father's heart and face,
manifesting itself in another's smiling delight,
and in the beauty of the world around us;
not invisible or indiscernible, but always there,
whether we see it or not.

Love is behind messages of support and hope
sent virtually by text or email but no less heartfelt;
the voice of a concerned passer-by
taking the time to check that we're OK;
the whistle of the eternal robin
that seems to linger always on the edge of our peripheral.
Love passes from our Saviour's heart and lips,
whispering from the mouths of others,
and the music of the world around us,
quiet but not inaudible,
the loveliest of sounds.

I CANNAE TALK LIKE YOU

I only have to open my mouth
to betray my status as an incomer.
If the accent doesn't do it,
then it's the subtle difference in dialect
that gives me away
for where you say *outwith*
I say *outside of*;
when I refer to *collection*
you call it an *uplift*,
and what I describe as *small*
is *wee* to you.

You can imagine my hesitation
when first asked, "Where do you stay?"
the phrasing indicative of temporary hiatus
rather than permanent residence,
and my uncertain response,
"I *live* here."

Before we moved
messages were received
by email, phone or word of mouth;
here folk go to the supermarket for them.

The cashier calls "First here"
(rather than "Next please"),
and if I ask for a sausage
it comes as a square,
not a cylinder or *link*
as it's termed.

And when it's raining
everyone comments on
how *dreich* it is.

I have *children*,

my friends here have *weans*,
and when we meet at the park
my two *take turns on the slide*
while the others *take a shot doon the chute*.

"Yes" still comes to my lips
more naturally than "Ay",
and I haven't yet had cause to exclaim
"Och aye the noo!"

I cannae talk like you,
and probably never will,
but yours is a bonnie language,
one I've always admired
and will always secretly envy.

CHURCH IS NOT HERE

Church bells no longer herald the way
for Sunday morning worship.
The pews are empty and the building
as quiet as a tomb, not even graced
by the rustle of angel wings.
A layer of dust has settled on the lectern
and the only light seeps in through the decorative glass,
staining the walls in a rainbow of colours
during brief moments of natural brightness,
a beauty for no living soul to see.

Church is not here anymore.
God's word has broken free
from stone walls and Sundays,
no longer confined to a place and schedule,
but timeless, omnipresent,
ever living in a world shutdown by disease.
The congregation has spilled out
through the open doors one last time
and scattered across the land
like tiny seeds of hope being sown,
taking root and beginning to grow.

NESTING DOLLS

in memory of Sheila Sparke

Four generations of women sit in a row,
ranging from two to ninety-two,

one sprung from the next like nesting dolls
but without the ability to return to the womb.

We are simultaneously different and alike;
a variation of the same blood flows through us

and our features all bear a resemblance
that's slightly altered through breeding,

disintegrating, fading with each lapse of time.
The beginning of this line is lost to us;

the women preceding us long pre-date our recollection,
and not one of us can predict where it will end.

But here we are, retrospectively: Sheila Myrtle,
Christine Shelagh, Kathryn Amy, Guinevere Saoirse.

Four generations of women together,
preserved for a moment in time.

PANDEMIC HIGH STREET

It's quiet, too quiet;
not dead exactly, but not bustling
with activity either.
There is a noticeable difference
in the stance of passers-by,
a hesitancy that wasn't there before
as they walk streets that are still familiar
but somehow not quite the same.
Shopping with confidence is now
a thing of the past.

They approach each destination
with uncertainty, carefully reading
the sign on the door to check
what's required of them,
silently counting the number of figures
already within, in case their entry
swells the number above what's
currently permitted at one time.
It's a maximum of three in the bank,
two in the pharmacy, but the
more spacious stores are less
concerned about specific numbers,
than they are about spacing them
appropriately along the aisles,
exercising crowd control Covid-style.

The lines on the floor, that indicate
the distance we should keep
from other shoppers, are already
beginning to wear away
and we're not even close to
the end of all this. Perhaps, in time,
we will automatically keep the correct
space between ourselves and others,
without the visuals to enforce this.

Waiting outside the bank, and bracing
myself against the biting autumn wind
that funnels up the high street,
I can't help but feel like a deathbed
visitor to a place once so full of life,
now given way to empty shops
and ever optimistic "To Let" notices.
The vital signs are present
and the heart beats feebly still,
but the overall outlook isn't good:
the high street is the next thing to be claimed
by an unrelenting pandemic
that's driven away the consumers.

CANDLELIGHT

Candlelight clears the head
from spectres of doubt and anxiety
that conspire to dim
the happiness and calm
we hold within.

The tiniest flame
wards them into the shadows,
dancing before our eyes,
a beacon drawing us
out from the darkness.

It will not fully illuminate,
nor will it stave off the draught,
but it welcomes us
into its warming presence
and casts its spell.

THE CENTRE OF THE UNIVERSE

My children argue over my right hand.
Compromise reached, I walk them to school,
weighted on either side as though by anchors,
so that I feel quite unbalanced
when I leave them at the door and walk home alone.
It's a wonder to me that the
umbilical cord isn't still attached.
There's a constant presence at my elbow;
to turn around too abruptly
runs the risk of treading on their toes.
They are always grasping, arms outstretched
for a perpetual cuddle that,
lovely though it is to be wanted,
doesn't always fit with what I'm doing at the time.
There are no secrets between us;
they even accompany me to the loo,
observing me without embarrassment,
watching me dress with open fascination.
This is what it is to be adored.

It's not easy being the centre of the universe,
but it's a universe that's constantly expanding.
Mostly, I recognise my position as a privileged one,
knowing that one day I'll be knocked off centre,
as my children grow more independent of me.
Then I will sit on the loo in peace,
turn around quickly to find no one standing directly behind,
walk along hands free all the time,
floating like a balloon and forgetting
what it was like to feel rooted to the ground.
And then I will realise how quiet the world is
without them always by my side,
my arms will feel so empty when
they're no longer revolving around me,
nor I around them.

OVER THE TOP

No guard duty for me – the days
of watching from a distant bench
are still some way off.
It's always over the top
and into the heart of the action,
the children leading me on.
They consider me a comrade,
despite the obvious differences in age and height
and I am flattered to be thought of as one of them.
They love having someone else to play with,
and when other children are about they are wild with delight,
following them around like some new and novel attraction.

That's not to say my role is made redundant
when other more desirable playmates are to hand;
if anything, I keep a closer vigil,
hovering nervously, when perhaps
I should step back and let them get on with it.
It's difficult to find that balance between
overprotectiveness and neglecting my duty,
when my child doesn't behave like the others,
and there's always a brooding judgement,
looming from the outskirts, or merely within my own head.

I suppose I am too quick to intervene;
apologising unnecessarily, or explaining away,
attempting to translate autism in the playground,
when it's a language I'm still learning myself.
I automatically anticipate our exile
because we are different, when really
personal experience should have taught me by now
to expect acceptance and welcome.
We are not among enemies, but allies,
for this isn't no man's land;
it never was.

CHRISTMAS PACKAGING

It's the time of the year that I drink Christmas blend coffee;
I'm always taken in by the Christmas tree motif against the
cheerful red,
forgetting the packaging is generally the extent of the festivity,
merely serving to disguise the mediocre cup of coffee within.

By mid-November Christmas is everywhere to be found,
Santa peering out from custard tins and cornflake packets,
glad tidings scrawled in witty puns across butter tubs,
and most unusually, the limited edition bleach,
because Christmas just isn't Christmas if your toilet doesn't
smell like winter spice.

It's the same at home.
We put up the tree the other day,
the same weekend the lights began to twinkle in the street;
started working through the Christmas flicks a fortnight
before,
about when we assembled the seasonal fruit cake.
The presents are mostly bought and now the wrapping
awaits,
along with several dozen Christmas cards to write and post,
and two wish-lists to send to the North Pole.

It's not about a baby in a manger anymore, if ever it was;
it's become a mish mash of Christian tradition, pagan ritual,
with goodwill to all mankind thrown in for good measure.

We do this every year, pull out all the stops
for the children or the child within,
ignoring the invitation to rest
in our vain efforts to kindle a glow that will endure
through the long winter ahead,

but rarely lasts a week beyond the turning of the year.

We forget it's in the stillness, in the quiet,
that the spirit of Christmas is ever present,
waiting to be discovered as we pause to reflect,
when we light a candle or stare out into the winter darkness
and feel the tingle of excitement within.

ACROSS THE MILES

The year is drawing to a close
and I sit here, trying to process
some semblance of it all,
to accompany the season's greetings.

We're all alive and well, which
is something to be thankful for
given the pandemic
we're currently living through.

The kids have endured it all
with remarkable stoicism;
not that they were likely to sniff
at the longest school holiday ever.

If anything, we're now more
appreciative of our immediate
surroundings; being at home hasn't
stopped us from having adventures.

We're all back at work and school now,
and adjusting to the changes
brought about, not that the world
has greatly altered in our absence.

We're taking life slowly, day by day,
looking ahead with an open mind,
trying to prepare for further change,
but holding onto hope nevertheless.

We didn't see you this year
and next year looks uncertain still,
but we're sending our love across the miles,
to remain with you in spirit

until the next time we meet.

YOUR ARMS

for Christine and Nick Ware

Your arms were the first to hold me
when I tumbled into the world head first.

Still warm and wet from the womb,
you lifted me up and drew me close,

an act that said more than words could:
that I was safe, that I was loved.

Time passed, and the arms that held so tightly
courageously let me go, miles away from you,

but always with the understanding
that I was welcome to return any time;

that under no circumstances
would I be turned away,

instilling within me a homing pigeon's instinct.
It's testament to you and your love

that wherever I go in life, to this day,
your arms will always feel like home.

Notes on Hope is Coming

I imagine 2020 has been a pivotal year for us all in some way or another, the global pandemic going a long way to alter the course of our lives during this time. For me, this was the year I discovered my voice as a poet, and it all began one sleepless night in January, shortly ahead of the outbreak of Covid-19 in our country. Lying awake in the small hours of the morning I was overcome with emotion, and giving up all pretence of sleep I got up and channelled this into my first attempt at poetry in a long time. *Recompense* virtually wrote itself; I had very little to do with it other than transcribing the lines as they formed in my head. With one poem behind me, another followed, and several more, and then Covid-19 happened, and in the midst of all the fear and change that suddenly surrounded us I found myself flooded with inspiration. Writing, for me, has helped me keep my head above water during a difficult period of transition to this change. All of the poems in this collection were written during 2020, apart from the first three. *Come What May* was written at the beginning of 2012, another defining year for me for various reasons; *When I Look at the Cross* was written in 2013 for the Magdalen Way Methodist Church newsletter; and *Blurred Photograph* was written in May 2019 to mark my son's fifth birthday. All of the poems in this collection have been printed more or less in the order they were written, so that although the subject matter varies from poem to poem, Hope is Coming presents itself as effectively my journey through this very trying year.

This collection would not have come about if it wasn't for the help and encouragement of several people. Firstly, I'd like to thank everyone who has followed and supported my dedicated Facebook page, Kathryn Epps Poetry. Your interactions with the material I've shared have given me the confidence boost I needed to get my poetry out there. Thank you especially to the Reverend Stewart and Avril Cutler, not only for encouraging my writing, but for featuring it, when appropriate, in the St Ninian's service and the quarterly Link magazine. Thank you to my parents, Nick and Christine Ware, and my husband, Lewes, for being the first readers of my poetry, and for all your constructive criticism. I'd also like to thank my Dad for his role as my publisher and to my husband, Lewes, for putting together the cover. And finally, thank you to my children, Timothy and Guinevere, for your endless inspiration and for always helping me to see the world in a different, brighter light.

Fiery Hedge Publications

Kathryn Epps Information:

https://www.facebook.com/kathryneppspoetry

Fiery Hedge Information:

https://www.facebook.com/fieryhedgepoetry

www.fieryhedge.wordpress.com

Other Publications on the Fiery Hedge imprint:

Nick Ware, Perception of Light (November, 2014)

Nick Ware, Subdued Anthems: Back Catalogue, Volume 1 (September, 2015)

Nick Ware, Strange Country: Back Catalogue, Volume 2 (November, 2015)

Nick Ware, The Beautiful Place (November, 2018)

Printed in Great Britain
by Amazon